ANCIENT EGYPTIAN CULTURE

By Katherine Gleason

Rourke

Publishing LLC

Vero Beach, Florida 32964

Developed by Nancy Hall, Inc., for Rourke Publishing.
© 2006 Nancy Hall, Inc.

Acknowledgments are listed on page 48.

www.rourkepublishing.com

Photo research by L. C. Casterline
Design by Atif Toor and Iram Khandwala

Library of Congress Cataloging-In-Publication Data

Gleason, Katherine.
  Ancient Egyptian culture / by Katherine Gleason.
     p. cm. -- (Discovering the arts)
  Includes bibliographical references and index.
  ISBN 1-59515-519-8 (hardcover)
  1. Art, Egyptian--Juvenile literature. 2. Egypt--Civilization--To 332
B.C.--Juvenile literature. I. Title. II. Series.
  N5350.G58 2006
  709'.32--dc22
                           2005010731

Title page: The Pyramids at Giza.
These famous pyramids were built as tombs for the
pharaohs Khufu, his son Khafra, and grandson Menkaura.

Printed in the USA
10 9 8 7 6 5 4 3 2 1

CONTENTS

OUT OF EGYPT

In this old photograph from the early 1900s, much of the Great Sphinx is buried by sand.

The **civilization** of ancient Egypt lasted for more than 3,000 years. This ancient culture is famous for its great art and architecture. Huge **monuments**, such as the pyramids, attract visitors from all over the world. **Mummies** have scared and fascinated people for centuries. The ancient Egyptians also created amazing carvings and built beautiful temples.

Ancient Egypt lay along the banks of the Nile River. Every year the Nile flooded, carrying fertile mud from deep inside Africa to the rocky desert shores of Egypt. The ancient Egyptians depended on this yearly cycle of flooding, drying up, and flooding again. Without the flood they could not grow crops. Other cycles, the daily rising and setting of the sun and the pattern of birth, death,

Found in Saqqara, this painted limestone statue of a scribe holding a papyrus scroll on his knees dates back to the fifth dynasty (2494–2345 B.C.E.).

and hoped-for rebirth, became important parts of the Egyptian religion.

Egypt was ruled by a king, also called a pharaoh. Egyptian **scribes** made lists of their kings, grouped in families called **dynasties**. The head of a dynasty usually passed the throne on to his son or daughter. Scribes noted the dates that each king ruled, but not all the lists have the same dates. So, in this book, the dates given for each king are approximate. **Archaeologists** have divided Egyptian history into periods. Each chapter of this book focuses on a different period.

CHAPTER 1

THE EARLIEST TIMES

(ca. 5300–3100 B.C.E.)

The earliest examples of Egyptian art are rock drawings of fish traps that are as much as 10,000 years old. By about 5000 B.C.E., the people of the Badarian culture had begun to grow plants for food. They made pottery bowls known as "ripple bowls" because of their wavy surfaces. They also carved small female figures from hippopotamus ivory.

The Naqada culture lasted from about 4000 to 3100 B.C.E. These people created small clay statues of women with upraised arms and small ivory figures of men with triangular beards. They

Pictures of boats and birds decorate this clay pot from the Naqada culture.

also made clay pots that were decorated with drawings of boats and women. **Palettes** for holding makeup were often carved in the shape of animals. These and other **artifacts** from Upper (or southern) Egyptian cultures were found in graves along with the remains of humans. By about 3500 B.C.E., the Naqada people had begun trying to make mummies by wrapping the dead in strips of linen.

Less is known about the people of Lower (or northern) Egypt. The artifacts of the Maadian culture have mostly been found in the ruins of homes. These people made simple clay pots and imported pots and palettes from Upper Egypt and from other areas.

The handle of this dagger from the Naqada culture is made of hippopotamus ivory. It is carved with battle and hunting scenes.

The ancient Egyptians may have been the first people to invent a writing system. Archaeologists have found **hieroglyphs**, pictures and symbols that stand for words or sounds, from as early as 3300 B.C.E.

CHAPTER 2

THE FIRST PHARAOHS

(ca. 3100-2686 B.C.E.)

According to legend, Upper and Lower Egypt were united by Menes, who founded the first dynasty, or family line of kings, in about 3100 B.C.E. In reality, Narmer was the first ruler. A beautifully carved slate palette from the temple of Horus at Hierakonpolis shows Narmer as the earliest king. On one side of the palette, Narmer wears the white crown of Upper Egypt, which is associated with the vulture. On the other side, Narmer wears the red crown of Lower Egypt, which is associated with the cobra. Later rulers wore both these crowns at the same time.

On one side of the Narmer Palette, Narmer, in the white crown of Upper Egypt, is about to strike and kill one of his enemies.

During this period, the names of kings were written inside a **serekh**, an image of a palace with a falcon on top. The falcon stands for the god Horus. A serekh was carved or painted on jars or labels, probably to show that they belonged to the ruler. Serekh have also been found on stone slabs in royal **tombs**.

The snake inside this serekh stands for Djet, Egypt's third ruler. It is carved in a slab of limestone that stood in the royal cemetery at Abydos.

The god Horus is shown as a falcon or as a man with a falcon's head. Horus is the son of Osiris, the king of the dead, and the goddess Isis. After Horus defeated the god Seth, he became king of Egypt. Horus was the most important god at Hierakonpolis, which means "hawk town." Over time, Egyptian rulers came to be seen as the living god Horus.

Pictures of Pharaoh Khasekhemwy's enemies are carved around the base of his statue.

In ancient Egypt, art had magical and religious power. To the people, a carving of Narmer killing Egypt's enemies did not just show the king keeping his country safe. It actually helped make sure that the country was safe. Because art had so much power, artists had to follow strict rules. Images of people were measured into 18 sections. The knees line up at the top of the sixth section, the elbows at the twelfth, and the shoulders at the sixteenth. The face, from the chin to the hairline, is two sections long.

One of the earliest stone statues of a king shows Khasekhemwy. According to a carving, he killed 47,209 enemies. Khasekhemwy's pose shows that he is ready to receive offerings, gifts of fruit, vegetables, meat, or perfume. The statues of kings were always carved to make them look perfect. That meant they also looked very much alike. So people could tell one king from another, the king's name was always carved on his statue.

Even though the feet are shown from the side, you can see the big toes of both feet in some reliefs. In life, you would see the big toe of one foot and the little toe of the other. In this relief from the tomb of the official Ptahotep (sixth dynasty, 2345–2181 B.C.E.), bearers carry offerings.

Reliefs, or wall carvings, often covered the insides and outsides of tombs. These images were there to help provide for the needs of the dead in the afterlife. People are shown with arms, hands, head, hips, legs, and feet viewed from the side, and the chest, eyes, and shoulders viewed from the front. Women are usually painted with yellowish skin, while men have reddish skin.

CHAPTER 3

THE AGE OF THE
PYRAMIDS

(ca. 2686-2160 B.C.E.)

King Djoser was one of the most important Old Kingdom rulers. He was buried in an underground room underneath a large step pyramid, which was designed by the architect Imhotep. Djoser's pyramid at Saqqara was the first pyramid. It was also the first really big stone building in the world. It stands 200 feet (62 m) high and has six steps.

Djoser's step pyramid

Djoser's pyramid is in the royal cemetery near Memphis inside a 30-foot- (9-m-) high stone wall. It's surrounded by an open court and stone buildings called **shrines**. Some of the shrines are stone imitations of Djoser's palace, which was built with wood. The court and the buildings were used during festivals that celebrated the king's power. The Heb-sed was a festival held during the king's 30th year of reign. The king had to run around a track and perform a dance, both to show that he was still strong and to renew his strength.

This statue of Djoser was found in a room on the north side of his pyramid. One wall had two spy holes so that Djoser's statue could look out at the stars.

Imhotep, the architect of Djoser's pyramid, came to be seen as the son of Ptah, the god of Memphis who ruled over art and art making. Imhotep was also seen as a god of wisdom and medicine. Although it is not true, many people believed that he was the first person to build with stone. He is shown holding a book-scroll, a symbol of learning.

13

The pyramids at Giza are not the only pyramids in Egypt, but they are the most famous. The Great Pyramid, which was built as a tomb for Khufu, originally stood 480 feet (146 m) tall and 754 feet (230 m) wide. (Because people have stolen stones, it is a little smaller now.) It probably took workers 20 to 25 years to build, but no one knows for sure how they moved the more than 2.3 million stone blocks into place.

Khufu's Great Pyramid (above right) is one of the Seven Wonders of the Ancient World. Though Khafra's pyramid (center) looks bigger in the photograph, it is not. All three pyramids were covered with a smooth casing of stones, which has all worn away except for a bit near the top of Khafra's pyramid.

Khafra, Khufu's son, built his slightly smaller pyramid near his father's. He also had the Great Sphinx cut from rock at the site. Over time, this giant statue of a crouching lion with the head of a man came to be seen as a statue of the god Horus. Menkaura, Khafra's son, built another, smaller pyramid nearby.

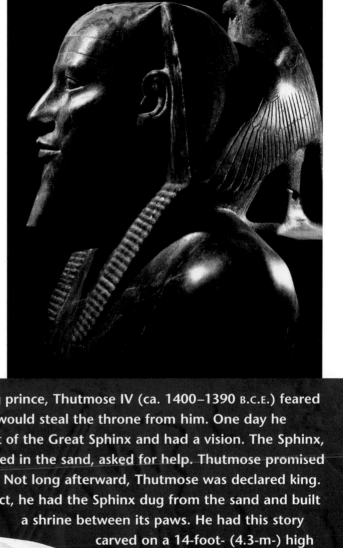

In this statue of Khafra, the falcon god Horus holds Khafra's head.

When he was still a young prince, Thutmose IV (ca. 1400–1390 B.C.E.) feared that one of his brothers would steal the throne from him. One day he stopped to pray in front of the Great Sphinx and had a vision. The Sphinx, which was almost buried in the sand, asked for help. Thutmose promised to do what he could. Not long afterward, Thutmose was declared king. In his first royal act, he had the Sphinx dug from the sand and built a shrine between its paws. He had this story carved on a 14-foot- (4.3-m-) high granite tablet, which was placed in the shrine.

Mastabas are low, rectangular tombs. The first ones were made for royalty. During the Old Kingdom, lower-ranking members of the court began to build mastabas for

The pyramid of Khafra looms over the mastaba cemetery at Giza.

themselves. Constructed from mud bricks or stone, each mastaba sat on top of an underground burial chamber. It had several rooms to hold food, furniture, clothing, jewelry, and other things the dead person would need in the afterlife.

Mastabas were built in great numbers near the pyramids. Their walls were decorated with reliefs or paintings of scenes from daily life. Some scenes show the dead person hunting, probably because this was something the person had enjoyed and hoped to do in the afterlife. Other paintings and reliefs, which show food being collected and prepared, were thought to magically provide food for the dead in the afterlife.

On the outside, mastabas have a painted or carved false door through which the dead person received offerings of food. Some mastabas have an image of the deceased standing in the door, but others picture him or her around the sides of the door.

A portrait of Iteti, an official, stands in the false door of his mastaba in Saqqara.

The geese painted on the wall of Atet's mastaba tomb at Meidum have become famous because of their natural-looking detail. Perhaps Atet, who was the wife of a high official in the court of Pharaoh Sneferu, liked to look at geese—or eat them.

CHAPTER 4

EGYPT GROWS RICH

(ca. 2055–1650 B.C.E.)

The Old Kingdom came to an end. Several princes divided Egypt and ruled their separate kingdoms for more than 100 years. Then King Mentuhotep II reunited the country and made Thebes his capital. All the arts grew in success and beauty. Many new buildings were constructed, including temples for the god Amun-Ra (also Amun) the main god of Thebes, and Mentuhotep's tomb at Deir el-Bahri.

Although little of it remains today, Mentuhotep's tomb was designed in a new style. It had terraces, walkways, and groves of trees. Instead of featuring Horus, this tomb had more images of the god Osiris.

In this statue, Mentuhotep's crossed arms and black skin imitate the god Osiris.

With the rise in power of non-royal people, special rites and blessings that once were given only to kings were given to ordinary people. Ordinary people began to be mummified and buried in coffins that were painted with great care and attention to detail. Few of these mummies have survived, but some of their coffins and masks have. Instead of featuring gods and kings, stories of the period, such as "The Tale of the Shipwrecked Sailor" and "The Tale of the Two Brothers," tell the stories of ordinary people.

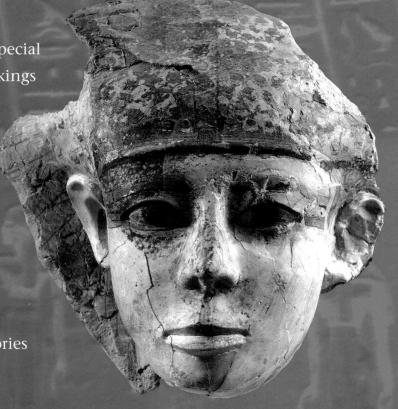

This painted plaster mummy mask from the 13th dynasty (ca. 1755–1630 B.C.E.) was found in Mirgissa.

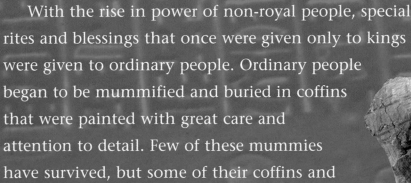

Osiris, the king of the dead and the father of Horus, was often shown as a mummy wearing an *atef*, the white crown of Upper Egypt with feathers on either side. Here, Osiris is pictured with a *hedget*, the white crown only, which also stood for rebirth. His skin is usually black, which stands for the fertile soil of the Nile, or green, which stands for the growth of plants.

During the Old Kingdom, carvings on tomb walls were meant to provide food for the dead person in the afterlife. During the Middle Kingdom, wooden models were left in tombs to take care of the needs of the dead.

These models showed people plowing fields, working with hoes, counting cattle, and carrying food such as bread, vegetables, fruit, and meat. They also showed things that the dead person hoped to enjoy in the afterlife,

Each of these models of a servant woman carries a basket of food on her head and holds a duck in her right hand. Like most standing Egyptian statues, each woman is shown with her left foot forward.

such as nice homes, gardens, boat rides, and musicians playing instruments and singing. The models tell us a lot about what life was like in Ancient Egypt.

Under Mentuhotep, **shabti** (or ushabti) figures, small human statues, were placed in tombs as well. At first, these figures were made from wax or clay. They were to act as a spare body in case the tomb owner's mummy was damaged. Later, the figures were crafted from **faience** (a type of fine pottery), wood, or stone and were used as magical substitutes. In real life, many Egyptians had to do work for the king. In the afterlife, when work had to be done for Osiris, the king of the dead, the shabti did it, leaving the dead person to enjoy an afterlife of leisure.

Wooden models of boats were found in many Egyptian tombs.

Jewelry reached a great artistic height during the Middle Kingdom. In 1894, a French archaeologist named Jacques de Morgan was working in the burial area of Amenemhet II at Dahshur. Two of the tombs de Morgan uncovered belonged to Amenemhet's daughters, Ita and Khnumet. Each contained several pieces of beautiful gold jewelry, including bracelets, rings, and necklaces.

This gold pectoral inlaid with carnelian and colored glass was found at Dahshur. It shows King Amenemhet III killing enemies under the outstretched wings of Nekhbet, the vulture goddess.

More jewelry from the Middle Kingdom was found in 1914 in the tomb of Princess Sithathoryunet at Lahun. Sithathoryunet was the daughter of Senwosret II, who came to the throne in about 1877 B.C.E. Her jewelry stayed safe from tomb raiders, who often stole everything of value, because it was hidden in a hole in a wall. Among her jewels were **pectorals** (decorations that were worn on the chest), girdles, wristlets, and anklets made from gold and semiprecious stones, including amethyst, turquoise, lapis, garnet, and feldspar. Much of the jewelry is based on images of wild cats. The precious materials used to make these pieces probably came from Nubia, a country to Egypt's south.

Egyptian jewelry from this time has also been found on the island of Crete and in Byblos, an ancient city in Syria. Some of the jewelry found in Byblos looks a lot like the pieces found at Lahun.

In 1894, Jacques de Morgan discovered this gold necklace inlaid with turquoise in the tomb of Princess Khnumet.

Ancient Egyptians often wore **amulets**, magical charms designed to bring luck or protect the wearer from bad things. Made from gold or precious stones, amulets were carvings of gods or sacred animals. The scarab was one of the most popular. It was an amulet of a dung beetle, which stood for the hope of rebirth in the afterlife. This pectoral belonged to KIng Tutankhamun.

CHAPTER 5

THE PEAK OF EGYPTIAN POWER

(ca. 1550–1070 B.C.E.)

The art and architecture of the New Kingdom may be the high point of Egyptian culture. After 90 years of foreign rulers, Egypt was reunited under Ahmose, Amenhotep I, and Thutmose I. Egypt became rich, many new temples were built, and old brick ones were rebuilt with stone. Queen Hatshepsut, the daughter of Thutmose I, was the first woman to call herself pharaoh. She was also one of Egypt's greatest builders.

In this large sphinx found at her tomb in Deir el-Bahri, Queen Hatshepsut wears a false beard, a sign of power.

Queen Hatshepsut's funeral temple at Deir el-Bahri was dedicated to the goddess Hathor.

Hatshepsut paid for amazing works of art and architecture, such as her funeral temple at Deir el-Bahri on the west bank of the Nile. Designed by Senenmut, the temple has large limestone ramps and terraces and is set off by the 1,000-foot- (305-m-) high cliff in the background. Carvings on the walls show Hatshepsut as the daughter of the god Amun-Ra, who by this time was considered the king of the gods.

Statues of Hatshepsut often show her as a man. She wears the king's kilt and headdress as well as the false beard that stands for power. To make herself even more famous, Hatshepsut had two 90-foot- (27-m-) high **obelisks** (stone pillars) carved from pink granite and placed in the temple of Amun at Karnak.

Amenhotep III was another great builder. In addition to having the huge temple of Amun-Ra built at Luxor, he had two enormous statues of himself made. Known as the Colossi of Memnon, they are among the largest statues ever built in Egypt, and they originally stood outside Egypt's largest funeral temple. After the statues were damaged by an earthquake in 27 B.C.E., one of them began to make noises that sounded like singing. Many

The Colossi of Memnon each stand 60 feet (18 m) tall and weigh about 1,300 tons.

people came to hear the strange sound, but when the statue was repaired in the third century C.E., the singing stopped.

Amenhotep III built temples all over Egypt. He also had the sacred Apis bull mummified and buried. Like most New Kingdom pharaohs, Amenhotep III was buried in the Valley of the Kings, a dry area in the mountains just west of Thebes.

The Apis bull lived in the temple of the god Ptah. It represented the god's soul.

The inner organs of a mummy were preserved separately from the rest of the body and stored in four canopic jars. These jars were sealed with carved tops representing the Sons of Horus. Duamutef, who had the head of a jackal, sat atop the jar holding the stomach. Hapy, who had the head of an ape, took care of the lungs. Imsety, with the head of a man, watched over the liver, and hawk-headed Qebehsenuef perched on the jar for the intestines.

The Ancient Egyptians worshipped many gods—Osiris, Horus, Isis, Hathor, Bastet, Amun-Ra, Ptah, and Thoth, among them. King Akhenaten broke with tradition and made everyone worship Aten, the disk of the sun. Akhenaten had all the temples of other gods closed. He built new temples for Aten, and a new capital city at Amarna. In ancient times, this city was called Akhetaten, which means "the horizon of the sun disk." Akhenaten's name means "spirit of the sun disk."

Relief carvings from the temples of Aten are very different from earlier reliefs. Akhenaten, his queen Nefertiti, and their children were carved sitting in informal poses, almost like snapshots.

In this relief, Akhenaten (right), Nefertiti (center), and their daughter Meritaten (left) worship the sun god, Aten.

In Amarna, artists used flowing lines and bright colors to paint scenes from nature on the walls and floors of houses. Literature, too, was written in a new style that used language that was closer to the way people spoke. Not everyone liked Akhenaten's changes. After he died, his name was erased from the list of kings. People called him "The Great Criminal" because he had closed the temples and thrown many priests out of their jobs.

A painted plaster floor scene from Akhenaten's southern palace at Amarna shows ducks flying up from behind plants that could be found along the Nile River.

People say that Queen Nefertiti, whose name means "a beautiful one has come," was one of the most beautiful women the world has ever seen. Even in the unfinished quartzite statue at left, her beauty stands out.

After Akhenaten's reign, Tutankhaten took the throne. Tutankhaten, who may have been Akhenaten's son or brother, soon changed his name to Tutankhamun ("living image of Amun"). He reopened the old temples and moved the capital back to Memphis.

Tutankhamun died young and was buried in the Valley of the Kings. The entrance to his tomb was covered with rubble from the building of another tomb. Because of this, Tutankhamun's is the only royal tomb that was not cleaned out by robbers in

Above: Howard Carter, the archaeologist who discovered King Tutankhamun's tomb in 1922, opens the sealed doorway to the burial chamber. *Left:* A modern reconstruction shows how a room in the tomb looked when Carter first came upon it.

ancient times. When it was found in 1922, people were amazed at the riches inside. Tutankhamun's mummy wore a mask of solid gold and rested inside four wooden chests nested one inside the other. These chests were nested in three gold coffins, which rested inside a **sarcophagus**.

In Tutankhamun's mummy wrappings were 140 amulets, carefully crafted daggers, and many pieces of beautiful jewelry. He was also buried with a jeweled throne made of silver and gold, statues, couches, chairs, board games, toys, food, linen clothing, and gloves. He had more than 400 shabtis, which were made of wood with gold appliqué, a kind of cut-out decoration, to do his work in the afterlife.

King Tutankhamun's solid gold mask is inlaid with semiprecious stones and glass.

Rameses II started another great period of temple building. He had old temples repaired and rebuilt. He also added to existing temples and sculptures, sometimes just by having his name carved on them. Beginning with Sneferu of the Old Kingdom, every pharaoh had his name written inside an oval called a **cartouche** that set off the royal name from other hieroglyphs. It was against the law for anyone else to write his or her name inside a cartouche.

Between 1964 and 1968, the two temples at Abu Simbel were cut from the rock and moved about 180 feet (54 m) so they would not be flooded by Lake Nasser after the construction of the Aswan High Dam.

Rameses was a warrior who, with his pet lion at his side, led the army to conquer Egypt's neighbors. He had huge statues and temples built to remind people of his successes in battle. One of his two temples at Abu Simbel in Nubia includes four 60-foot- (18-m-) tall statues of the king. Cut into the rock of the cliff, this temple extended almost 200 feet (61 m) into the earth. Rameses's memorial temple near Thebes, known as the Ramesseum, also has enormous stone statues of the seated king.

Rameses II's name written in hieroglyphs inside a cartouche

No one knows what their music sounded like, but tomb paintings are proof that ancient Egyptians enjoyed it. In this wall painting, Inherkhau and his wife, Webet, smile as they listen to the music of a blind harpist. Inherkhau was head of the craftsmen at Deir el-Medina during the reigns of Rameses III and his son, Rameses IV.

CHAPTER 6

AN EMPIRE (ca. 1070–664 B.C.E.)
DIVIDED

Egypt was divided again. Early in the period, the high priest of Amun-Ra at Thebes ruled over the south, and a king named Smendes ruled in the north. The pharaoh, no longer seen as the son of a god, became less important in religion. Amun was thought of as the true king, while the living king was just someone who worked for him. Egypt lost control of Nubia and other lands that had made the country rich. Almost all of the New Kingdom tombs at Thebes were taken apart, their stones and metal reused, their treasures stolen, and their mummies reburied in groups.

Like Sheshonq II's, many royal coffins were made with falcon heads.

Artists created many beautiful works of art from different kinds of metal. They used gold to make amazingly detailed statues of Amun. To craft the falcon-shaped coffin of Sheshonq II, they used silver. And to make the statue of Queen Karomama as a goddess in a religious ceremony, they used bronze.

Women became more important in religion, holding the titles "first great chief of the musical troupe of Amun" and "god's wife of Amun." In reliefs found at Karnak, god's wife is shown doing things that only kings used to do—making offerings, being embraced by gods, and receiving symbols of kingship from the gods. A fragment of a relief from North Karnak even shows "god's wife" celebrating a Heb-sed festival.

The daughter of a pharaoh of the 22nd dynasty (945–715 B.C.E.), Karomama was appointed to be the wife of the god Amun. Her bronze statue is inlaid with pink gold, silver, and glass paste.

Funeral practices changed during this period. Instead of each mummy having its own tomb, people were buried in family groups. Guards found it easier to protect one group tomb from thieves than to protect a lot of separate tombs.

The tombs were simpler and without decoration, but artwork covered the coffins, both inside and outside. Instead of burying furniture, clothing, and other items with the mummies, artists now painted the items on the coffins. They also included

In his coffin painting, Ankhefenkhonsu is offering papyrus and lotus flowers to the god Osiris. On his head is a perfume cone. More commonly worn by women, perfume cones were made of wax. As the wax melted in the heat, it ran down over the head and shoulders, scenting the skin.

pictures of gods that had once been painted on the tomb walls. They sometimes applied the paint to a thin layer of a plaster-like material called **gesso**, which has a smooth surface that paint sticks to. The coffins were also decorated with metal and inlaid stone, and sometimes made in the shape of a mummy.

Henettawy was called mistress of the house and chantress of Amun-Ra. The painted decorations on her outer coffin imitate the jewelry, gold, and precious stones that covered the royal coffins of earlier times.

Maat was the goddess of truth and order. She led the dead person to the Hall of the Double Maat where his or her heart was weighed against a feather, Maat's symbol. Only a person that lived well and so had a light heart could be reborn in the afterlife. On the shabti chest at left, the gods Anubis and Thoth weigh the heart of the deceased, while Horus looks on.

CHAPTER 7

THE LATE PERIOD

(ca. 664-332 B.C.E.)

Again, Egypt went through a time of trouble and warfare. In 664 B.C.E., Psamtek I reunified the country and built forts to defend it. Persian leaders ruled as Egyptian kings from 525 to 404 B.C.E. and again from 343 to 332 B.C.E. Egypt's traditions of art and architecture continued. Great funeral palaces, such as the one for Mentuemhat in Thebes, were built for officials. Artists often copied the work of earlier times, while adding their own original touches. Sculpture, especially in bronze and faience, reached a new height of beauty and craftsmanship.

In earlier times, special animals, such as the Apis bull of Memphis, were held sacred. Cows in general, though, were not sacred. During the Late Period, that changed. For

When Thoth appeared as a baboon, he was known as the Keeper of Light. As an ibis, he was linked with law and writing.

example, all cats came to be seen as sacred to the goddess Bastet, while all ibises were sacred to Thoth. When a sacred animal died, it was mummified and buried in a special cemetery. The festival of Bastet, which was one of 60 holidays celebrated in a year, was held at her temple in Bubastis. Thousands of people came by boat to listen to music, dance, and drink beer.

The goddess Bastet was often shown as a woman with a cat's head.

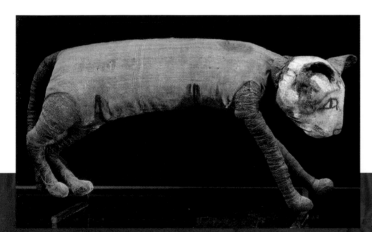

In 2002, veterinarian Douglas Cohen used X rays to examine a cat mummy owned by the Albany Institute of History & Art and discovered that the mummy was really a dog. Animal mummies often were faked. Sometimes the mummies turn out to be a few carefully wrapped bones, or, in a few cases, just a lump of mud. The cat mummy above, however, is real.

This bronze statue shows the
goddess Isis nursing her son Horus.

In 51 B.C.E., Cleopatra VII, the last Ptolemy, became ruler of Egypt and fought against the Roman Empire. Cleopatra, who was a single mother, was compared to the goddess Isis, another single mother, whose son was Horus. The area of Alexandria where Cleopatra lived is now under water, but in 1996, explorer Frank Goddio found her palace buried in mud just 18 feet (5.5 m) down.

In 30 B.C.E., the Roman emperor Augustus conquered Egypt. He had the Temple of Dendur, which honors Isis, built in the Egyptian style so that the local people would like him.

In C.E. 384, the Roman Emperor Theodosius, who was a Christian, had most of the Egyptian temples closed. The last hieroglyphic carving was made

The elegant temple at Philae may be the most beautiful of all Egyptian buildings.

in C.E. 394 at Philae in the sanctuary of Isis on an island in the Nile near Aswan. Philae was the last Egyptian temple to stay open. In 395, the Roman Empire was divided into the Eastern Empire and the Western Empire. In 476, the Western Empire collapsed, and by 646, ancient Egypt had come to an end.

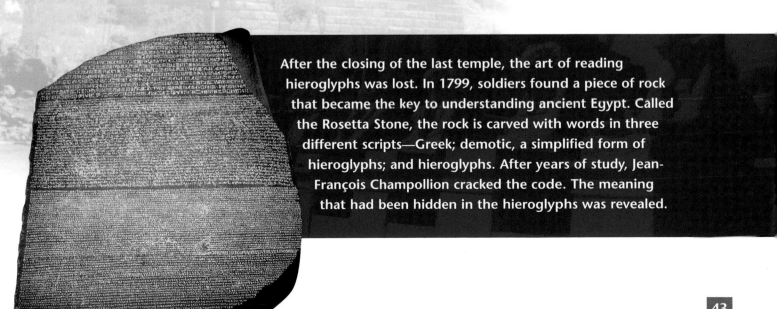

After the closing of the last temple, the art of reading hieroglyphs was lost. In 1799, soldiers found a piece of rock that became the key to understanding ancient Egypt. Called the Rosetta Stone, the rock is carved with words in three different scripts—Greek; demotic, a simplified form of hieroglyphs; and hieroglyphs. After years of study, Jean-François Champollion cracked the code. The meaning that had been hidden in the hieroglyphs was revealed.

Predynastic Period (ca. 5300–3100 B.C.E.)

5000 Badrian people begin to grow crops

4000–3100 The Naqada culture

3500 The Naqada people wrap the dead in linen strips

3500 Earliest known hieroglyphs

Archaic Period (ca. 3100–2686 B.C.E.)

3100 Egypt united under Narmer, the first pharaoh

?–2686 Reign of Khasekhemwy (last king of second dynasty)

Old Kingdom (ca. 2686–2160 B.C.E.)

2667–2648 Reign of Djoser

2613–2589 Reign of Sneferu

2589–2566 Reign of Khufu

2558–2532 Reign of Khafra

2532–2503 Reign of Menkaura

First Intermediate Period (ca. 2160–2055 B.C.E.)

Middle Kingdom (ca. 2055–1650 B.C.E.)

2055–2004 Reign of Mentuhotep II

1911–1877 Reign of Amenemhat II

1877–1870 Reign of Senusret II

1831–1786 Reign of Amenemhat III

Second Intermediate Period (ca. 1650–1550 B.C.E.)

New Kingdom (ca. 1550–1070 B.C.E.)

1550–1525 Reign of Ahmose

1525–1504 Reign of Amenhotep I

1504–1492 Reign of Thutmose I

1479–1425 Reign of Thutmose III

1473–1458 Reign of Queen Hatshepsut

1400–1390 Reign of Thutmose IV

1390–1352 Reign of Amenhotep III

1352–1336 Reign of Akhenaten

1336–1327 Reign of Tutankhamun

1279–1213 Reign of Rameses II

1184–1153 Reign of Rameses III

1153–1147 Reign of Rameses IV

Third Intermediate Period (ca. 1070–664 B.C.E.)

1070–1043 Smendes rules in the north

ca. 890 Reign of Sheshonq II

Late Period (ca. 664–332 B.C.E.)

664–610 Reign of Psamtek I

525–404 First Persian Period

343–332 Second Persian Period

Greco-Roman Period (332 B.C.E.–C.E. 395)

332–323 Reign of Alexander the Great

305–285 Reign of Ptolemy I

51–30 Reign of Cleopatra VII

30 B.C.E.–C.E. 14 Reign of Augustus

379–395 Reign of Theodosius

amulet a charm worn as protection against evil or injury

archaeologist a person who finds and studies objects from peoples and cultures of the past

artifact an object remaining from an earlier time period

cartouche an oval that contains the hieroglyphs of the name of a ruler

civilization a high cultural level that includes a writing system and written records; also, the cultural group that has achieved it

dynasty a family that holds power for several generations

faience a fine glazed pottery, usually colored green or blue

gesso a mixture of plaster and glue used as a surface for painting

hieroglyph a picture or symbol representing a word or a sound in the ancient Egyptian writing system

mastaba a rectangular tomb

monument a memorial building, statue, or other lasting reminder of a notable person or event

mummy the body of a person or animal that has been preserved after death

obelisk a tall piece of stone carved to have four sides and a pyramid-like point at the top

palette a thin board or slab of stone used for mixing colors of paint or makeup

pectoral a piece of jewelry worn on the chest

relief a carving, usually on a wall, that is made so the figures stick out from or sink below the surface

sarcophagus a stone coffin

scribe a person whose job is to write or to copy text by hand

serekh an image of a palace with the name of a king inside and a falcon, which represents Horus, standing on top

shabti a small human figure that was buried with a mummy to do work for the mummy in the afterlife; also ushabti

shrine a sacred place, tomb, or container

tomb a grave, room, or monument for the dead

Ancient Egypt Revealed by Peter Chrisp, DK Publishing, 2002

Cat Mummies by Kelly Trumble, Clarion Books, 1999

Cleopatra by Diane Stanley, HarperTrophy, 1997

Mummies by John Malam, Kingfisher, 2003

The Pharaohs of Ancient Egypt (Landmark Books) by Elizabeth Payne,
    Random House Books for Young Readers, 1981

Pyramid by David Macaulay, Houghton Mifflin/Walter Lorraine Books, 1982

Pyramid (Eyewitness Books) by James Putnam, DK Publishing, 2004

The Riddle of the Rosetta Stone: Key to Ancient Egypt by James Cross Giblin, HarperCollins, 1993

The Shipwrecked Sailor: An Egyptian Tale with Hieroglyphs by Tamara Bower, Atheneum, 2000

Web Sites

The British Museum
Ancient Egypt
http://www.ancientegypt.co.uk/menu.html

Carnegie Museum of Natural History
Life in Ancient Egypt
http://www.carnegiemuseums.org/cmnh/exhibits/egypt/

CHICO
(Cultural Heritage Initiative for Community Outreach)
University of Michigan, School of Information
Mummies of Ancient Egypt
http://www.si.umich.edu/CHICO/mummy/

ACKNOWLEDGMENTS

The editors wish to thank the following organizations and individuals for permission to reproduce the images in this book. Every effort has been made to obtain permission from the owners of all materials. Any errors that may have been made are unintentional and will be corrected in future printings if notice is given to the publisher.

Cover: Mummy cartonnage with gilded mask, Greco-Roman period (332 B.C.E.–C.E. 393) from Fayum, Egypt/The Art Archive/Private Collection/Dagli Orti
Title page: Ablestock
Contents: Photograph © Jean Berko Gleason
p. 4: Library of Congress
p. 5: Seated scribe, painted limestone, ca. 2475 B.C.E., Old Kingdom, fifth dynasty, Saqqara/The Art Archive/Egyptian Museum, Cairo/Dagli Orti
p. 6: Red-figure vessel, Predynastic Period, Naqada culture, Abydos/The Art Archive/Egyptian Museum, Cairo/Dagli Orti
p. 7 (right): Dagger, Predynastic Period, Naqada culture, Gebel el-Arak/The Art Archive/Musée du Louvre, Paris/Dagli Orti; **(left):** Ablestock
p. 8: The Narmer Palette, schist, Archaic Period, Hierakonpolis (Kom el Ahmar)/The Art Archive/Egyptian Museum, Cairo/Dagli Orti
p. 9 (right): Djet, ca. 2980 B.C.E., bearing the serpent hieroglyph (the phonetic value for which is djet) framed by a serekh (palace façade design) and surmounted by a Horus falcon, limestone funerary stele, Archaic Period, first dynasty, Abydos/The Art Archive/Musée du Louvre, Paris/Dagli Orti; **(left):** Ablestock
p. 10: Seated statue of Pharaoh Khasekhem with conquered foes incised around the base, Hierakonpolis, Dynasty II, c. 2700 B.C. (limestone), by Ashmolean Museum, University of Oxford, UK/Bridgeman Art Library
p. 11: Offerings bearers, bas-relief from mastaba of Ptahotep, Old Kingdom, sixth dynasty, Saqqara/The Art Archive/Dagli Orti
p. 12: Ablestock
p. 13 (top): Djoser, limestone statue (detail), Old Kingdom, third dynasty/The Art Archive/Egyptian Museum, Cairo/Dagli Orti; **(bottom):** Imhotep, bronze, Late Period/The Art Archive/Egyptian Museum, Turin/Dagli Orti
p. 14: Ablestock
p. 15 (top): Head of Khafra, Old Kingdom, fourth dynasty, Giza/The Art Archive/Egyptian Museum, Cairo/Dagli Orti; **(bottom):** Ablestock
p. 16: Pyramid of Khafra with mastabas of fifth and sixth dynasties in foreground, Giza/The Art Archive/Dagli Orti
p. 17 (right): False door of Iteti, limestone, Old Kingdom, sixth dynasty, Saqqara/The Art Archive/Egyptian Museum, Cairo/Dagli Orti; **(bottom):** Geese fresco from mastaba of Atet and Nefermaat, Old Kingdom, fourth dynasty, Meidum/The Art Archive/Egyptian Museum, Cairo/Dagli Orti
p. 18: Mentuhotep II, painted sandstone statue, Middle Kingdom, 11th dynasty, Deir el-Bahri/The Art Archive/Egyptian Museum, Cairo/Dagli Orti
p. 19 (top): Mortuary mask, painted plaster, Middle Kingdom, 13th dynasty, Mirgissa, Sudan/The Art Archive/Musée du Louvre, Paris/Dagli Orti; **(bottom):** Osiris, stone (detail), Late Period/The Art Archive/Egyptian Museum, Turin/Dagli Orti
p. 20: Procession of offering bearers, painted wood, ca. 1950 B.C.E., Middle Kingdom/The Art Archive/Musée du Louvre, Paris/Dagli Orti
p. 21: Large painted boat model, wood, Middle Kingdom/The Art Archive/Musée du Louvre, Paris/Dagli Orti
p. 22: Gold pectoral inlaid with carnelian and colored glass belonging to Mereret, sister of Amenemhat III, Middle Kingdom, 12th dynasty, Dahshur/The Art Archive/Egyptian Museum, Cairo/Dagli Orti
p. 23 (top): Gold and turquoise collar belonging to Khnumit, daughter of Amenemhat II, Middle Kingdom, 12th dynasty/The Art Archive/Egyptian Museum, Cairo/Dagli Orti; (bottom): Gold pectoral with semiprecious stones belonging to Tutankhamun, New Kingdom, 18th dynasty, Thebes/The Art Archive/Egyptian Museum, Cairo/Dagli Orti
p. 24: Sphinx of Hatshepsut, New Kingdom, 18th dynasty, Deir el-Bahri/The Art Archive/Egyptian Museum, Cairo/Dagli Orti
p. 25: Temple of Hatshepsut dedicated to Hathor, New Kingdom, 18th dynasty, Deir el-Bahri/The Art Archive/Dagli Orti
p. 26: Photograph © Jean Berko Gleason
p. 27 (top): Painted limestone stele showing Apis, New Kingdom, 20th dynasty, Memphis/The Art Archive/Musée du Louvre, Paris/Dagli Orti; **(bottom):** Canopic jars, painted wood, Third Intermediate Period/The Art Archive/Musée du Louvre, Paris/Dagli Orti
p. 28: Akhenaten, Nefertiti, and daughter Meritaten, alabaster, New Kingdom, 18th dynasty, Amarna/The Art Archive/Egyptian Museum, Cairo/Dagli Orti
p. 29 (top): Painted plaster floor scene, New Kingdom, 18th dynasty, Amarna/The Art Archive/Egyptian Museum, Cairo/Dagli Orti; **(bottom):** Nefertiti, quartzite, New Kingdom, 18th dynasty, Amarna/The Art Archive/Egyptian Museum, Cairo/Dagli Orti
p. 30 (top): Howard Carter (1873–1939) using crowbar to open sealed door in tomb of Tutankhamun, 1922/The Art Archive/Culver Pictures; **(bottom):** Reconstruction of antechamber in tomb of Tutankhamun, New Kingdom, 18th dynasty, Thebes/The Art Archive/Pharaonic Village, Cairo/Dagli Orti
p. 31: Photograph © Jean Berko Gleason

p. 32: Ablestock
p. 33 (top): Cartouche of Rameses II, New Kingdom, 19th dynasty, Temple of Luxor/The Art Archive/Dagli Orti; **(bottom):** Fresco of harpist and listeners, tomb of Anherke, New Kingdom, 20th dynasty, Deir el-Medina/The Art Archive/Dagli Orti
p. 34: Silver coffin of Sheshonq II, Third Intermediate Period, 22nd dynasty/The Art Archive/Egyptian Museum, Cairo/Dagli Orti
p. 35: Statue of Karomama, bronze inlaid with pink gold and silver, glass paste eyes, Third Intermediate Period, 22nd dynasty, Thebes/The Art Archive/Musée du Louvre, Paris/Dagli Orti
p. 36: Sarcophagus painting of Ankhefenkhonsu, Third Intermediate Period, 22nd dynasty/The Art Archive/Egyptian Museum, Cairo/Dagli Orti
p. 37 (top): Outer Coffin of Henettawy, Third Intermediate Period, Dynasty 21, reign of Psusennes I, ca. 1040–992 B.C. Egyptian; From Deir el-Bahri, western Thebes; Gessoed and painted wood; H. 79 7/8 in. (203 cm)/The Metropolitan Museum of Art, Rogers Fund, 1925 (25.3.182) Photograph © 1992 The Metropolitan Museum of Art; **(bottom):** Shabti chest belonging to Shawenhwy, painted wood, Third Intermediate Period, 21st dynasty/The Art Archive/Musée du Louvre, Paris/Dagli Orti
p. 38: Statuette of Thoth in the form of a baboon, faience, Ptolemaic Period/The Art Archive/Musée du Louvre, Paris/Dagli Orti
p. 39 (right): Statue of Bastet with head of cat, bronze, Middle Kingdom, 12th dynasty/The Art Archive/Musée du Louvre, Paris/Dagli Orti; **(left):** Mummy of cat, Ptolemaic Period/The Art Archive/Musée du Louvre, Paris/Dagli Orti
p. 40: Photograph © Jean Berko Gleason
p. 41: Mummy cartonnage with gilded mask, Greco-Roman Period, Fayum/The Art Archive/Private Collection/Dagli Orti
p. 42: Statue of Isis suckling infant Horus, bronze, Ptolemaic Period/The Art Archive/Collection Antonovich/Dagli Orti
p. 43 (top): Photograph © Jean Berko Gleason; (bottom): Rosetta Stone, The Art Archive/British Museum/Dagli Orti
Background, **p. 4:** NASA
Backgrounds, **pp. 6, 8, 41, 44:** Ablestock
Background, **p. 14:** Library of Congress
Backgrounds, pp. 19, 23, 27, 28, 34, 43 and all sidebar backgrounds: Photographs © Jean Berko Gleason